C000201163

Vanessa Kisuule is a rising star of British poetry. She graduated from Bristol University with a Bachelors in English Literature and currently splits her time between writing poetry and making coffee for people. Both have the capacity to make people happy – which is always the dream. She has won several slams including Farrago School's Out Slam 2010, Poetry Rivals 2011, Next Generation Slam 2012, and SLAMbassadors 2010. She has performed at Glastonbury, Lounge on the Farm, Secret Garden Party, Wilderness and Shambala festivals. She has also performed in pubs, unkempt back gardens, in dingy kitchens and attempted to get out of paying a bus fare by shouting poetry at the driver – it worked! She has completed commissions for London's Southbank Centre and Bristol City Council and written two plays and two one woman shows, *Flesh* (2013) and *Love and Other Highly Regarded Fictions* (2014). In 2013 she was voted Best Performance Poet in both the Sabotage Reviews Saboteur Awards and the inaugural South West Poetry Awards.

Joyriding
the Storm

Vanessa Kisuule

Burning Eye

This edition published by Burning Eye Books 2014

www.burningeye.co.uk

@burningeye

Burning Eye Books
15 West Hill, Portishead, BS20 6LG

ISBN 978 1 90913 629 8

"There are these two young fish swimming along and they happen to meet an older fish swimming the other way, who nods at them and says, *Morning, boys. How's the water?* And the two young fish swim on for a bit, and then eventually one of them looks over at the other and goes, *What the hell is water?*"

David Foster Wallace

To Vanessa Cooper – you were at my first ever poetry open mic. And the rest, as no one says, is miraculous mystery. I am forever unworthy of your friendship and my words perpetually inadequate to describe the dizzying wonder that is you.

CONTENTS

Jjajja

I do not know you
I have composed you from
Dress cotton
Banana leaves
Patchwork quilts of quiet smiles and stories
That I could not understand
As I hold your hands
I know they've known more work in this past hour
Than mine will in their entire lifespan
I see the hardship of a thousand winds
Blowing across your face
So I trace a map of apologies
Across the fault lines of your fingers
And hope some amorphous ghost
Of my meaning lingers

You're a goddess
Your shoulder blades press together
Where your wings once met
And yet
We can only exchange
Awkward nods of acknowledgement
Because my world cannot slot into yours
Though I crawl on all fours
For meagre scraps of my identity
Endlessly grieving every mistranslation
Misunderstanding
Misinterpretation
Each seismic shift in time
I'm inventing you
Through a generation gone by
And as we sit in silence
Seedlings of the same wizened tree

I can imagine
I'd tell you of the short skirts girls in England wear
And the joys of Jeremy Kyle
How snow falls
Like capricious cotton balls of bliss
On nights cold as an Eskimo's kiss
I'd ask of the past
The laughter shared
The songs once sung
What Mum was like when she was young
If I weren't trapped with the handicap
Of my British tongue

I envision the talks we'd have
Tucked in the candlelit cave of a power cut
Cradled in a clash of culture
Hoping the Tower of Babel might bleed into oblivion
And somehow
A tainted miracle might unfurl
I'm willing to bet
We'd have been the best of friends
In a different world
But I do not know you
I've composed you from
Dress cotton
Banana leaves
Patchwork quilts of quiet smiles and stories
That I could not understand
In this land of lost language
I am neither stranger nor native
The weight of my wasted words
Cannot be translated

*Jjajja: Luganda for 'Grandmother'

14

Strawberries

Strawberries always remind me of you
Sweet red flesh of squandered summer days
The bizarre novelty of the word boyfriend
Tingling on my lips
There were plums
Rhubarb and raspberries on your parent's farm
Ripe and blushing like a bride slowly and softly undressed
But I liked the strawberries the best
I'd eat them by the punnetful
And always felt sick afterwards
I gorged on them so that when their season ended
I wouldn't miss them so much

I was sixteen then and my virgin lips had yet to be kissed
I felt like a freak
Floating face down in a jet black abyss
PS thanks for pulling me out
You were ever so white and small and skinny
We looked silly together but I didn't care
Because when I spoke you listened
As if my voice were the chorus to your favourite song
And your lovely eyes more than made up for your lanky arms
You'd read a lot of books and knew a lot of stuff
That was enough for me
You were like my teacher
One that I could make out with
Behind rhododendron bushes at house parties

But we argued incessantly
Mainly over whether Bob Dylan or Aretha Franklin
Were the more superior artist
I was stood in Aretha's corner
Holding up her heavenly wail of molten gold

Holding up her heavenly wail of molten gold
Like a shield of sheer unadulterated awesomeness
You retaliated by making me listen to Dylan
Some anaemic hunk of a hippy
Who wore Rayban shades indoors
And had a voice that made me crave Strepsils
Bob Dylan I said *is a glorified poet with delusions of musicianship*
Aretha Franklin you said *never wrote a note of what she sang*
She had mediocre albums and occasional hits
It was an argument rendered obsolete
By how fundamentally different the two are
The underlying metaphor was lost on us
But I didn't budge and you didn't budge
And now we're just friends who talk occasionally
And I listen to *Blowin' In The Wind* constantly
Not so much because I miss you
But more because I can now concede that sometimes I'm wrong
That sometimes I'm difficult and cruel and obstinate
Unwilling to let *like* ferment into other L words

I was constantly comparing what we had
To what I'd seen in movies
Heard in songs
And read in Shakespearean sonnets
Our adolescent ambivalence always fell short
When we kissed
I simulated the sensation
Of my heart skipping a beat
It almost felt real
But I wanted crush to be an operative word
All the clichés bursting into Technicolor
Pushing me to my knees
I wanted to feel your hands

Clasped round the rungs of my ribcage
Holding on for dear life
I wanted my stomach to ache
When you weren't with me
Like an overexcited child
Who's eaten too many strawberries

Strawberries always remind me of you
And how I'll always be writing *like* poems
And lust poems
And *what was all that fuss* poems
Never love poems
But that's not your fault or mine
Blame Hollywood
Blame high hopes
Blame Motown's marshmallow rhymes
And though we're no longer together
And your voice is fainter than a whisper
Across a barren field in bleakest winter
I still imagine
Against all odds
Bob and Aretha sat on a bench somewhere
Singing in perfect harmony
Their voices melding into endless possibilities
As they share a punnet of big
Red
Juicy
Strawberries

The Carpet

Don't curl your toes like that
You're messing up my hairstyle
It takes a while
To organise these threads
Into this distinctly nonchalant cross hatch
Suppress the urge
To morph my fibres into six inch spikes
That could
Should I wish it
Sink into the firm flesh of your feet
But I am soft and submissive to your touch
I make no sound
Floorboards creak in protest
Water runs rejected on kitchen tiles
Whilst I
Wear indelible dents from the press of table legs
Bruises from cheap red wine after candlelit dinners
Living is an abusive business

But I see you
When your feet
Still damp from a shower
Drag across me
Two rotting fruits hanging
From a long suffering tree
I see your private dance for the mirror
You do not writhe and thrust
In your usual mating display for faceless names
In sticky clubs and dark parties
You are angular and frantic
Joyously ugly
More honest than you will ever be
Outside these four walls

I am a soaked sponge of midnight sin
No whip round with the Hoover
Or cheap Afghan rug will muffle me
The secrets I keep sit deep
But one day they will wrestle free

Remember that
Next time you walk all over me
As casually as if I were made of mere clouds
Or dreams

The F Bomb

You say that you are tired
Tired of feminism
Women's rights
Women talk
General woman-ness
Its relentless shouting
Growling vengeful spitting hunger
Bra burning penis squeezing barbarism
Its frequent tendency to piss on the campfire
Ruin the party
Its awkwardness
Its
Irrelevance
And you know what?
I'm tired too
More tired than you could ever know
Worn and weary and bored
Of woman
As status symbol,
A dagger to be plunged into people's chests
An excuse
An apology
Or political statement
I would much rather it were just a description

I am tired of going to parties
And wishing my skin into a silk
Velvet or studded leather
Something to protect me
From the eyes that trespass across my skin
Breath always held
Tongue always tucked under itself
I hesitate

Stutter
Stultified
Don't let them hear your heart
Fluttering inside your pathetic
Paper prism of a chest
Get back in the kitchen woman
Make me a sandwich woman
Don't frown
Pipe down
Woman
We're all post-modern
Witty young people so
Laugh at the joke
Woman
Until the paper prism starts to tear at the corners
And the tears course down your cheeks
Salt shame slick as an oil spill
I don't want to be the one
To throw the F bomb into the room
Its explosion dull yet thunderous
Leaving a sulphurous smell in the air

 am tired of shoving
Every man and boy I meet into a box
A box so small and stifled
That they surely cannot breathe
Through the cancerous green of my jadedness
Forget about the supposed epiphanies
Found tucked in the waistbands of jeans
Littered inside the sheets of ruffled beds
I want to watch box sets
Take a guided tour inside your head
I am tired of tearing beautiful girls

Into confetti beneath my trembling fingers
Sprinkling them over the licking flames
Of my insecurities
Assuring myself
She is probably not very clever
That every boy must surely want
To tuck themselves into the parentheses
Of those dimples
Run their fingers through those whisper strands of hair
And hating her for it
I am tired of staring until my eyes sheen over
Peeling dissecting dismembering rating out of ten
Circling flesh to crimson with haemorrhaging pens
I would like the word beautiful
To unfurl from my tongue
As an observation and not an accusation
I am tired of solitary fingers
Pointed like unloaded guns
At men at magazines at mothers
At the very sky above my head
I want to splay my fingers out
And raise them above me
Like I were catching snowflakes
Or second chances
Like maybe
One day there will be men and women
But most importantly just people
People made up of tear ducts
Bruises and faint memories
Of a ghoulish time when half the world
Lay flat under the foot of the other
Voiceless
We will laugh

And shake our heads in mild horror
That things could have ever been that way

You tell me you're tired of holding back
Fearing the next thing you say
Could be the wave to crash across the shore
Unsettling everything indefinitely
Funny
We have that in common
You tell me you are tired
And you know what
I'm tired too
More tired than you can ever know

For The Record

Perhaps you do not understand
What you are dealing with
And who is to blame you
Soft brained whirlwind that you are
You are unfamiliar
With a breeze as calm and constant as this
I have been trained in the twisted art
Of digging symphonies from aching gulfs
Some nights rang louder than a god's scream
Hurled across the night sky
But now I've grown a taste
For the black honey of your absence

You are no more than a slipped stitch
In a sprawling tapestry
You may think that you have drowned me
But I still dance in puddles in bare feet
After the sky has wept the day dry
I will save my balled fists
Raw throat and aching eyelids
For a moment worth punching
Screaming and crying for
My darling
This is not it
But please
Continue to imagine that I am pining
Clutching at breath from the ghostly grasp
Of your hands on my heart strings
Whatever keeps your ego warm
On those particularly frosty December mornings
I can no longer fill your gaping mouth
With lyrics to love songs
That you will never know the words to

We were surely made for better things
Than to be puppets
Or fumble fingered masters
Tangled in knotted strings

One day you will meet someone
Who you would walk across naked flames for
I only hope they would still kiss
The soles of your charred feet
And not recoil
Overwhelmed and ashamed
But I
Cannot burn for you this way
Not whilst there is a whole world
Unpeeling itself for me
An impossible swell of souls
To be teased from their cracked shells

Go on your way without guilt or pride
I will be here with no umbrella or raincoat
Counting raindrops
And even as they drench my skin
Seep into the dark earth
I know that from this
A quiet shoot of infinite chance must grow

Nurturer

(for Sam, Lin, Kav and Coop)

I know those hands
Palms perpetually pointed upwards
You tenderly unwind the leathery rind of the world
Pull it apart into segments
For others to eat
Still warm from your fingers
That splay out like sun rays
There is almost always never any left for you
Only the residue of something so precious
You couldn't bear to keep it to yourself
You are not like the others
You love like a thunderstorm
Relentless rain that leaves puddles
Gleaming with oily rainbows
You know deep down
That you cannot protect everybody
But still you extend yourself
Infinitely thin and wide

Taken for granted
Your ears fill with worries that could drown a fish
The worn shelves of your shoulders
Stacked with the old cracked stories
Of our sadness
I am like so many others
I love like an amoeba
Single celled absorption of everything around me
You swell me up to ten times my size

Some will claim to care for you
When they are devastating
Bloodthirsty and insatiable

They love with fat leeching hearts
Saying your name
Like a twisted anagram of their own
Siphon off the nectar of your kindness
Your goodwill runs thickly through their veins
An alleyway drug for the listless

How many times have people loaned you their tears
So you can sprinkle your own salt through them
Wear them on your own cheeks until their owner
Grows the courage to claim them back?
How many nightmares have you sown inside your eyelids
So the ones you love can sleep easy at night

We call you the nurturer
A dying breed of people who live
To make others happy
You are always loaning out your smile
Attaching it to others
Telling them how much
It suits the frame of their face
But it is yours
No one wears it quite like you

Aftermath

Afterwards
They will turn my pockets inside out
Unfold the dead bus tickets
With the hushed reverence of a suicide note
Roll the lint between their fingertips
Imagining I once did the same
Fashioning the miscellaneous grey pellets
Into bullets
They will read my diary entries
Simpering sixteen year old sentiments
Thin and fleeting as a slip of the tongue
Noting how my ls and ts slant like a drunken man
Tightrope walking along the edge of a crooked pavement

They will run their fingers along my CD collection
Looking for metal and menace
The insistent bass thrum
Of grinding teeth and razor blades
They will find nothing
Other than a Deluxe Edition of Fleetwood Mac's Rumours
Hardly touched soft rock albums
Bought as well meant birthday presents

They will comb through the ragged threads
Of my frayed existence
Looking for a father or uncle or neighbour or distant cousin
Who placed his hands where they shouldn't have been
Enquire as to whether I played violent video games
Worshipped NWA or Slipknot
Wrote self-hating haikus
On Post it Notes stuck to my bedroom mirror
They want to know that I am a special case
That it takes a lot of wringing

Pulling
Stretching
To make something twist and writhe
Inside itself so passionately

They will fashion their own nails and nooses
Prostrate my memory onto a cross that I never carved
No one thought to ask me how or why
I had permanently balled fists
Crescent moons in my doughy palms
From the nails that I never cut
They do not know that blind hatred
Is a cloak that some wear tentatively
Only to eventually shrug it off
While others wrap it round their shoulders
Huddle under it
Slowly feel its raw silk against their fingers
They do not know what it is
When people look right through you
As if the final draft of your obituary were written
On the greying paper of your face
They want to know that I'm a special case
That it takes a lot of wringing
Pulling
Stretching
To make someone twist and writhe
Inside themselves so passionately

But I know that as they lay in their beds at night
It is not me that they fear
But the difference between us
How very small and unconsidered it is
The sweet terror they must feel
As they look down at their hands
And see how they could curl round the curve
Of a trigger
Or a soft throat
As easily as reaching out like a dying man
Begging for someone to grasp onto you
As your ribs coax the fire in your chest
That eats every last morsel of hope
In its path

Crayon

The kid holds a crayon like a last chance
I ask what he is drawing and he quickly shakes his head
I suddenly see the irrelevance of the question
His Playdoh heart has not furled
Into a pulsing fist of fear
The crayon has not been seized from his clammy palms
Not yet
Dot to dots are mere suggestions to him
Round and menacing
Like the garden peas he refuses to eat at dinner time
Finite full stops on the ends
Of prison sentences
He sees past their constellation of conformity
Anarchy travels in wobbly lines
He imagines
Puddles of noise and colour that beg to be jumped in
Spun sugar skipping ropes that swing to infinity
Not even the paper
Instigates limit or boundary
His crayon etches its joy
Past the A4 and across the table
Waxy trails in the grooves of the wooden desk
He switches to felt tips
Inks the ends of Nora's pigtails and gingham dress
A Crayola shade of chaos
I ought to have stopped long ago
Had the knot of envy in my stomach not been so tight
His tongue rests in the gulf
Where his front teeth once were
As he grins a grin that could turn dust into glitter
You can't do that kid I tell him
I hand him a fresh sheet of paper
A sharpened HB pencil

I follow the numbered dots
With scissor blade precision
He takes the pencil and copies me
Diligently
I walk back to my desk and pick up my pen
Fighting the urge to bite into my own skin
Scribble all over the magnolia walls
Remembering when crayon wax collected
Beneath my fingernails
As if I had gripped onto the world with both hands
And refused to let go

Sex Education Class

The trajectory of a sexual awakening
Feels less like a revelation
And more like waking from a blissful sleep
In an unfamiliar bed
A tourist in your own body
A little girl playing dress up
In high heels too big for your feet
Do you remember the first time
You felt a hand on your bare skin
Suddenly aware of being inside something
Meant for more than housing blood
Guts and playground games
The most terrifying realisation
A not quite kid can ever have

Why does nobody warn you
How much your walk can change
How every bit of you permanently tingles
With expectation
There was a code of silence
A code we all pretended we understood
We bought lace bras
Turned our stumbles into struts
Called each other sluts
Until it felt like a compliment
Girls swapped virginity stories like Pokemon cards
There were rumours of bushes
Public toilets
House parties
Littered with the stones of popped cherries
The words *not yet*
Sucked from swollen Lolita lips

Everyone is having sex
They said
An inordinate feverish web of sexy sex
I longed to be a six second centrefold spread
In the lad's mag of malevolent minds
I wanted my own piping hot slice of the lie
To scald my tongue on the heat of desire
My own words of protest silenced to ash
A crematorium for conflict
I sought the touch of strangers
Let them map out their territory
Surely they felt it
The thickening lava under my colonized skin

Once again
I press my lips to the thick liquor
Of whimsical fantasy
I want to Viennesse waltz
Eat pancakes off bare chests
Do unspeakable things in the backs of cars
Whisper black magic
Onto lips unlocked with mutual trust
The illness of romance
Seeps pink and putrid into gasping pores
I lock myself away
So even I can't find the key

The Incidental Sister

Shitbags
Weird wailing jellyesque little shitbags
I knew you would suck up time and space
Like parasites
Cunningly disguised
In matching Mothercare pastel blue babygros
I'd been an only child for fourteen years
I was good at it
I didn't get that much attention
But at least I didn't have to split the air around me
Into equal parts to share around
I only had my mother to fight with
For sovereignty over the remote control
That was the life I knew
I woke up to it sure as the mattress
Beneath my back every morning
But my mother remarried
A man I met a week before the wedding
My head had barely stopped spinning
And you were already growing
They had had sex – actual sex
I was shocked and horrified
At the proof growing inside her stomach
Like a bloated question mark
I did not know what to do
So I did nothing
Told no one
And pretended it wasn't happening
It took me a few months to unfold my arms
And reshape them into a cradle of acceptance
Which you could fit into
But you did
Perfectly

Your fingers were marvels
Silken fronds of chalk seaweed that gripped
Firm as iron
You smelt clean and new
I rested my nose in the crook of your neck
I imagined it must be the scent
Of nirvana on laundry day
It was then that I became
Your incidental sister

But now you're far too heavy for me to carry
You seem to grow taller by the hour
You can recite your eight times table
Which by the way I still struggle with
But sometimes you will wonder
Why people don't understand you
Whether you speak a different strain of English
I remember now how strange and difficult it was
You are two black pebbles in a blanket of snow
The other kids will only have seen faces like yours
On Oxfam adverts
Do not worry
You will get used to it
Try not to boil with frustration
When they tug at the coils of your hair
And ask how it stands up on end like that
Remember you will say plenty
Of ignorant things in your lifetime too
And Mum
Mum may seem like a tower
Taller and stronger
Than anything you could ever build with your Lego bricks
But she folds like tracing paper

And sometimes she even crumplesBut she will only do it while
you are asleep
And dreaming of aeroplanes and space rockets
I bet she wishes she could escape sometimes too
Make her a cup of tea on occasion
The traditional way in a thin plated saucepan
No matter how hard we try
We will never understand the extent of her sacrifice
No one has invented a measuring device
That can span the sheer width of it yet
You will struggle
In being boys and men but mostly human beings
But you have what I never did
Each other
Partners in crime and confidence
Playing catch is so much easier with one other person
Take it from someone who knows
Scrabble, chess and life
Aren't as fun to play on your own
I'm in the middle of writing you a book of advice
On the backs of envelopes
Scrap bits of file paper
Off white pearls of wisdom, if you will
But I don't say all this
From a lofty platform of self-assurance
Sometimes getting out of bed in the morning
Can feel like re-learning how to walk and talk
And trust
In many ways I am still a newborn
Only without the cool bits
The gossamer skin and pebble toes
I want you to know that I am there
All the time

Though you may not know it
I think of how you evolved
From parasites to princes
Part of me wishes
You could have stayed cradle shaped
Forever
But I know that you must be big and tall
And fully formed
To do all the small and awesome things
That you were surely destined for

Clifton Suspension Bridge

As I stand by Clifton Suspension Bridge
I imagine what it would be like to jump off it
Not because I'm suicidal
I'm as happy as any person can deliberately be
But despite this
I envision my mind steeped in a darkness
So thick and tight
That the sun is no more than a distant mockery
The whistling of the air between my arms
As I smash my fists against the door of death
Demanding to be let in
It is then I know I want for nothing more
Than the miracle of breath and blood
The audacious press of life against lung

I peruse death casually
Wondering if it might suit me
A slightly loud pair of patterned trousers
Screaming from a shop window
Fascinating and terrifying
What is the texture of that kind of nothingness
It is like sleep
Fuzzy and cushioned
An ironic return to the comfort of the womb
Or is there a heaven after all
And indeed a hell
Can either of them live up to all that hype
I ponder it as if life were a distraction
From the real business of oblivion

As my friends stand beside me
Talking of the view
The nice bistro pub by the hills
And what to have for dinner
All I can see is the Samaritans Plaque by the wall
I look down and down and down
Feeling a delicious twinge of foreboding
Death I thought
It's all the way down there
And I'm all the way up here
I'm sure there's some significance in that
We don't stay much longer
The sun is setting and we are hungry

I don't remember what we had for dinner
But we did go back to that bistro pub
On another day
There was a view of the bridge from the window
It took my breath away
It really did
For five whole seconds
I counted

Walking on The Moon

When I told people
I wanted to walk on the moon
They nodded
Muttered things about NASA and Neil Armstrong
While I piled up pound coins
One on top of the other
Forgoing my usual trips to Sainsburys
For Curly Wurlys and Starburst sweets
In favour of a pilgrimage to the CD store
Where I bought your albums
Collecting them like other kids did
Stickers and knee grazes
You were gold dust to me
From the first time my aunty played your music
From a record collection that climbed up
Well above my five year old head
I could feel it in my bones even then
I could not get my head around how one body
Could hold so much magic and enigma
Aunty I would ask
How does he stand up on his toes like that
Will I ever move like that one day
Why is his face white in that picture
And brown in that one
I wore your CDs to scratches and dust in my Walkman
You taught me a lot
That I wanted to find something
And be dizzyingly brilliant at it
Sparkle as bright as a pair of diamante socks
You taught me that we are vultures
Creating false gods from the fallible and fragile

Only to tear them from their thrones
With our bare teeth
We will not stop
Until we have the flesh of a dead corpse
Hanging from our pulsing mouths
The camera bulbs will flash all the while
Televise the demise of dignity and good taste
I remember that day
It didn't feel real and it still doesn't
It is the closest I have come to death
I can only imagine how it will feel
When it snaps its jaws around one of my own
My mother
The toughest woman in the world
Came back from the office saying
She had been fighting back tears all day
I have not much more to say other than this
Michael
I miss you
No I didn't know you
But you are there
Indelibly threaded through my childhood
As sure as story books and hair bobbles
Though I don't believe in God or Heaven
Or retribution
I think of you sometimes
Scaling the surface of the moon
Laughing singing and dancing
Literally and figuratively
Out of this world
PS

Every winter I buy cheap woollen winter gloves
That manage to stay a pair for a matter of weeks
Before I lose one
I am forced to walk through the chill
With a glove on one hand
And a balled fist with the other
I don't mind it so much
I like to think it is you me and the cosmos
Sharing our own private little joke

Flesh – an excerpt

Matrophobia: The fear of turning into one's own mother.

I read that word in an article in one of those magazines you get in the weekend paper. And you know what I thought of? Yesterday when I walked past the open door of my bathroom and caught you staring straight back at me. A ghostly fist clenched in my chest and I dropped the boiling mug of tea in my hands onto my bare feet. It didn't even occur to me jump away from the scalding spray of liquid. The burn seemed to register in some distant peripheral horizon of my brain. I reached out for you, dumbstruck. How had you managed to sneak so stealthily into my bathroom and wait for the moment when you could catch my heart as it tumbled from my mouth. But of course, it wasn't you. It was just my mirror reflection playing old, worn tricks on me.

It was always the way. Every party, gathering, wedding and Christmas the aunties would make a ceremony of clasping my face between their thumb and forefinger and swing my head left, right, left 'Gweh! Look at this one. Just like her Mummy. You know you look just like your Mummy?' And I would stand there listless, permanent craters cutting into my cheeks from the long false pincers on the ends of their fingers. They'd linger a little too long, waiting for a response from me when all I could do was stare and hope you or Dad would be round the corner with a glass of something cold and sweet. You would save me from any more scrutiny, shoo me away so the grown-ups could talk big, tall talk and I would be free to scamper away with your heavy shadow draped across my back.

Even Aunty Rahima, who knows me as well her own children, used to say she felt that she'd stepped into a time machine when she looked at me. Like surely she was fifteen again and you were both sat face to young, grinning face rubbing cocoa butter into each other's faces, whispering made up witches spells under their breath. Sketching blunt edged stars and swirls on the inside of their thighs, buttered sunshine collecting underneath their nails. Buttered sunshine. That's what we would call it, as Jjajja told you when you were children. There are special people whose job it is to climb their way up the sun's rays and scrape stolen sheets of light from its surface to be softened into a cream that can turn the scaliest skin into midnight silk. These sheets of sun are hot. Hotter than a hot comb as it accidentally brushes the top of your ear, hotter than a pot of stew straight off the stove, hotter even than the metal engine of a motorbike against bare skin. The sun scrapers are said to have skin that crumbles on contact like a moth's wing. They cannot love other humans the same way they once did because the sun has blinded them. Everything and everyone else seems dull and colourless in comparison. Their hands glow the colour of burnished heartbreak, a glaring testament to the loneliness of love. Buttered sunshine. Is it silly that I still call it that? That even at the age of thirty seven I worry the residue left on my hands might erode my skin while I sleep, that I will wake up in the middle of the night to the acrid smell of frying flesh? As I rub it into my own daughter's cheeks every morning I think of those lovelorn sun scrapers, how they shimmer with the unique burn of one sided love.

I had yet another awkward phone conversation with Dad today. He was his usual non-commital self, harrumphing and coughing into that long suffering handkerchief of his. He started anecdotes and let them dangle unfinished across the phone line, sighing like a man who always sees the rust on a silver lining. I could hear the absence of you in every laboured inhale of breath, every attempt at pretending that everything was just as it always was. I was frustrated with him, that silly, heartbroken old man. Angry that he could fall apart with such soft ease, that grief could fill a mouth with such wordlessness. But then the guilt came, regular as clockwork. I made false excuses about dinners burning in ovens and hung up. Dad's strange ways never bothered me as much as they did then. But after I had put Lena to bed, I sat curled up in the armchair, sat on my hands to keep them from trembling. I dug into boxes of old things and feelings, looking at pictures of you in the old photo albums with the cracked corners. You had a smile like a unicorn stood in the midst of Brixton market. Startling. Teeth like ivory, piano concertos tingling under your lips. Strong, elegant arms like a ballet dancer's. Your collar bones stuck out like two cocked rifles. No breasts or buttocks forming rounded brackets on the straight sentence of your body. You looked like a warrior. I remember your pride that you stayed slim and sturdy as a metre ruler through three pregnancies, our pot-bellied bodies sliding from you as a fluid and seamless as a choreographed dance. Not like my experience of giving birth: a twenty two hour labour, a Caesarean scar across me from where Lena was pulled from my sighing stomach like silk scarves from an amateur magician's hat. Her eyes screwed shut as she wailed in protest, I realised someone had ripped the roof of her quiet, liquid house from above her. I ached with love and pity. Remorse. I wanted you there, to be strong and silent for the both of us, to wipe the endless fluids coating Lena's skin and matting my hair to my head, to assure me I hadn't pulled my child from the one place she would always be safe.

Aunty Rahima smelt like a failed experiment. When she hugged me I was scared to rest my head on her shoulder, the scent of her made my nostrils burn like the barrel of a gun. Her skin was mottled, dirty pink brown. It made me think of the pigs on the farm we had visited on a school trip, how they looked nothing like the yummy sheets of breakfast that would sizzle and hiss in Mum's frying pan on Sunday mornings. God had coloured Aunty Rahima in with the wrong crayon. Her hands and face were light as the dawn but the true midnight of her lingered on her knuckles and knees. I'd watch her in the bathroom drawing in her eyebrows with a dark pencil, combing through her lashes with mascara until they all pointed up like a fan of exclamation marks across her eyes. And then the final ritual: she'd reach for the pink tub of cream with the picture of the ghost woman on it. She'd scoop the cloud white stuff on the tips of her fingers and rub it into her cheeks, across her forehead, down her slanting pyramid nose. The ghost woman on the tub was not smiling. She watched over Aunty as she massaged the cream into her face until it disappeared into her skin like snow into parched earth.

Now I don't know what crazy is. I don't know if it is mad to see my dead mother in my reflection. I cannot talk to John about this. My husband approaches all corners with a pair of sharp scissors. As far as he can see, if something is severed then it is solved. He slices any mention of you from conversation, tells me I must not wallow or indulge myself. Entire years have gone past, he says, I must remember that I am a mother first and a daughter second now. He is right, I suppose. He handled the death of both his parents with a soldier's silence I both envy and fear. Can I talk to you about John, Mother? Now, now that you're dust in the ground can I acknowledge what you saw and what I chose to ignore over fourteen years ago? How his eyes constantly seek a light that he doesn't see in my eyes but in the women at his workplace. That charm I know all too well on full display at all those garish work functions he drags me to, where I, mortified, sit in my cheap and sexless M&S shift dress watching him place coded secrets in the small of a silk haired, slim hipped woman's back. He drives us home afterwards, telling me how sweet and smart Lucinda is, how we would get on so well. She's originally from Norway, don't you know? Do you remember when you had a figure like hers, Hilda? Not that you aren't still beautiful, not that you aren't still attractive, my darling. Just something that crossed my mind. He compliments me when I come back from the hairdresser's with a long, light weave that he can stroke with his large, tree bark brown hands. Don't you feel like a woman, Hilda? I love you with hair like this, he says. He came home one day with a box of child's

47

relaxer for Lena, told me she must be presentable for her first day in school. You understand, Hilda. The kids at this school do not know what hair like hers looks like, they will tease her and make her feel ugly. She must fit in with the other children. The girl on the picture has the same frozen eyes of the ghost woman, but she is smiling too big and too wide. I tell him no. No, John. She is too young. He sighs, loosens his tie as he sits down on the overstuffed sofa. You know, he tells me, Lena is not a bush child and she will not be raised as such. The women in my family are sophisticated. Aristocracy. They do not carry the dust of Africa underneath their fingernails like a legacy from the gutter. They have toilets that flush, they eat at French restaurants and wear Gucci to buy vegetables at the market. Their hips are slender and their hair is as a proud woman's should be. What do you think we are, Hilda? We can't be common and vulgar like these mzungu people wish us to be. They expect you to be broad hipped and clumsy, thick tongued and charcoal skinned with hair like a rag doll. This is not a matter of aesthetics Hilda, but of pride. My face is hot, my lips do not recognise the shape of my anger. I pick up the pink box and rest it on a high shelf in the bathroom and tell him we will talk about it later. At night, he touches me beneath the duvet and I feel the curve of Lucinda's neck on his fingertips, he kisses me everywhere other than my lips for fear I taste her on him and, Lord help me, mother, I love him for that small, inconsequential demonstration of mercy. He is not a bad man. He loves me and his child in his own scissor bladed way. He saw something in me that no other man did. Him, with his whitened teeth and six figure salary, tailored suits and talk of upward mobility and points to prove. I will not betray him. I just want him to stroke the wool on his daughter's head and tell her that being a ghost is not the only way of shining in the dark. Then I will forgive him anything. I will not need to tell him of the time that I found the number of a golden haired prostitute in his briefcase. How I called this woman and asked her her name and age, found out she had a Masters in

Anthropology and a seven year old son. I told her she had a beautiful body. I will not tell him how I told her that I fantasised of watching my big, black husband being fucked by a blonde, white woman, seizing her by the thighs and making a blasphemous alter of her angelic flesh. How I told her to tell me what she did to him, every detail. How I hung up before she could tell me anything. How I sat for an hour with the phone in my hand in the lounge, calm as the silence before a bomb blast. I needed you then, Mother. But all I had was your uncanny likeness staring back at me from the blank TV screen.

I stayed at Aunty Rahima's for two nights just before Christmas to keep her company in that small, sad box of an apartment. She looks awful now. Not the sassy, loose limbed big sister you knew. She is even paler now. The tubs of cream she uses are strong, counterfeit potions with foreign lettering across them. I saw them resting by her toothpaste and cocoa butter in the bathroom cabinet, nestling awkwardly like an unwanted guest at a party. She buys them in unlicensed beauty parlours where pineapple haired witch women reign behind the counters. But I felt her love for us in her tight embrace, her cupping of my face with her gentle papery hands. We sat and talked about you, in a way I can't with Dad or John. We drank cheap wine and remembered you like a friend that wasn't gone, just hadn't rung in a while. She told me about the first time you and Dad met, how you could only laugh at a man who owned five beige polo shirts. How you'd never known a boy to love so quietly before. No words or promises so big and coarse that that they drag across the ground. He just listened to you, cared for what you had to say, played endless games of chess with you. Always had his palms upwards in anticipation of yours. 'People laughed at the two of them together, Aunty said. 'This woman swallows him whole, their friends would say. African men and their pride. Like a wall they just refuse to see past for fear there's only air behind it. I'm sure you know this more than most. But your father is a pillar, though, my dear. He has not much to say for himself because he knows how to just be. Why do you think we all talk such incessant nonsense at each other, telling people 'I am this, I am that'. As if we were confirming it with ourselves every day. Not your father, dear. He just is.' And I thought of him, coughing up his last years into his handkerchief, the five minute silences stretching across the phone line. How he used to sit me in his lap to learn the rules of chess at the age of five and you would look on, calm yet incredulous. I know that feeling now. The sheer impossibility of us humans all interconnected even whilst we sit marooned in our shells and minds and cells. I went to bed that night determined to call Dad the next day to invite him round for a game of chess that I might even let him win.

I woke up to Lena tugging at my arm at nine in the morning. I do not usually sleep past eight but the wine had me drowsy, even as I opened my eyes I could taste the previous night's wonkiness on my tongue.

'Mummy. Mummy!' she says.

I say, 'Leave Mummy alone, she's sleeping now,'

She says, 'Mummy please. Buttered sunshine.'

I opened my eyes a fraction. Confused. Why is she talking about cocoa butter with tears in her eyes. I see her face and familiar smears of un-rubbed moisture on her skin.

'Mummy, the buttered sunshine. Aunty bathed me and she told me to go in the cupboard to find the buttered sunshine.'

'Okay. Good girl. You need to rub it in properly, I can still see it on your face.'

'This doesn't feel like buttered sunshine. Mummy, this one burns.'

I open my eyes. There is an angry white smear all across Lena's body. Her eyes stare out at me, unblinking. She is a ghost.

Lena has rubbed the stuff all over her body, down her face and neck and up into the nook of her inner thighs. I am swiping at her poor, defenceless skin too hard, too forcefully. I am silently screaming words that are not words. I am scaring my little ghost child into silence thick as untouched snow. Her skin is singing a white nightmare that I cannot wake her up from. I wipe the cream from her cheek with a scooped palm to find burnt pink underneath. Her raw pink flesh glowing through the singed skin, she is burning in worship to a false god and I am powerless to stop it. And why are you not here? I need your presence, cool and calm as a glass of water. I am calling an ambulance with trembling fingers, terrified at the sight of Lena's tearless face. I wipe at her face and limbs with a damp towel as we sit mute on the drive to the hospital in awkward, choked panic. I am taken back to the last time I saw your face. A long, sterile corridor, long as your arm extending outwards, your hand cupped in the shape of a way out. I see it now, Mother. What you saw all along. We are all foolish, fawning sun scrapers, going to touch the surface again and again, fooling ourselves that one day we will not be met with pain but redemption. And yet we continue to burn. We no longer recognise what we look like without a crown of flames.

Mother, what am I do to when I come from a lineage of women perpetually on fire?

Brick Dust

Your body is a house. For better or worse this is where you live. So needless to say, you should have no desire to engage in love affairs with pyromaniacs, redecorators, graffiti artists, squatters or cavemen who wish to use the staircase of your ribs as kindling. Sometimes you may find your own face amongst the throng of demolitionists at your door. People will bring flowers to your gate but you may not be ready to let them in. You may still be far too afraid of wasps hiding beneath petals. But wave from a window so people can see that you are there and that you are trying your best. Soon you shall welcome the right guests with open arms. Look forward to that day. We're all just trying to make homes from brick dust.

Reinventing Religion

I tried to create my own god once
From the debris on the cutting floor
Of everyone else's feathered faiths
I think she is a woman
Though she could be a man if she wanted
Or a jellyfish
A snow leopard
An amoeba of caprice
She'd have all the good parts of the other gods
But she'd be a little bit fucked up
Not as relentlessly glorious as all the others
Teeth made from nunchucks
Charcoal dust nails
She'd speak in rock and roll clichés and smoke rings
Scars between her breasts
Breath like the tail end of a stormy night

I started to sketch out her flesh and mould her voice
But dipping my fingers in the fantasy
She changed shape inside my palms
The disobedient clay of her
Coating my fingers in a new and horrifying mud
She was supposed to be the god that wouldn't fail me
And this quasi-worship would have been something
Other than this fudge thick emptiness

Some days I reach out for the child I once was
The girl who prayed with the belief
That truth and hope swing from the same gallows
The God with a capital G
Stained the clouds with His looming shadow
They told me He loved me

But He was no fun
A faceless reprimand who built the world
From thunder and guilt
Sometimes I wished I could bite into Bibles
Taste the stigmata fresh from that boy man's palms
A twisted kind of communion
The church had no space for my breed of carnivore
So I peeled myself away
I was free of scripture and hellfire for a while
But now I float with nothing to pin me down
Sometimes I miss the conjured voice of higher reason
If not divine then at least beautifully crafted

But instead
I tried to create my own god once
She rests precariously
On a slanting shelf in my subconscious
I am waiting for a single hand
A mere gust of wind
That will inevitably come and knock her over
Smashing her to irretrievable shards
As numerous as my doubts
As jagged as my crooked intentions

Playground Debt

Even now
I struggle to remember his name
But I remember his eyes were dark
As half remembered dreams
Drowned in shame
A stormy sky just before
It starts to pour with rain
Sometimes he'd be behind me
In the lunch queue
Smelling like snot and PVA glue
Like boys tended to in those days
At playtime
He'd sit all alone
In a corner of the playground
So serene and still
Not making a sound
He looked like he kept on awful lot of thoughts
In such a little head
I grew an irrational fear
That they might start to trickle
Like treacle from his ears
Justine
The undisputed queen of the under seven scene
Made a beeline for you that time
St Michael's slightly chubby answer
To Regina George
She gorged on your silence
Your secrecy
Your solitude
They began to sing
At first just Justine and her followers
Burst forth with a ditty on you
The dirty dithering Paki

From what I could tell
The song was spontaneously sparked
Yet surprisingly catchy
A soaring chorus
For any insecure kid to latch onto
Dirty dithering daydreaming
Paki
The group of singers grew bigger
A cancerous catcall
Of kids kicking footballs
Crunching crisps
Laughing and joking in euphoric bliss
And even now
I struggle to remember the words of the song
Exactly
But he sat as they spat out that word
Paki
Picked up off parents' tongues
And scraped off street corners
His face twisted in a stoic refusal to show any pain
Nevertheless the stormy skies of his eyes
Started to rain
I stood there
Entranced by the song
And its tribal dance
It didn't occur to me
To condemn their gluttonous glee
So relieved was I
That they weren't singing about me
The bell rung and the song was sung
We went on with our day
That was the last I saw of him
The boy with all the thoughts and no name

And even now
Fifteen years on
I struggle to scrape the shame from my skin
I was a kid
I was lonely
I was lucky
Pick your excuse
Apologies in hindsight
Are always conveniently profuse
Cowardice comes in many colours
A rainbow of regret over my head
For the mistake I cannot mend
The boy I didn't defend
I know I have no right to know how his story ends
But I hope he's some place
Where his thoughts sprouted wings all the same
Some place where people sing his praises
And everyone knows his name

Twitter Poetry

He said the word love
Like a sweet plucked at whim from a bag
That he now could not wait to spit out.

*

As anyone in this sugar rust city knows
The casual yet precise rolling of a cigarette
Is the finest form of origami.

*

I am patient
Bring me a man who will run his fingers down my back
Like the cracked spine of his favourite book.

*

She wears a red bow in her hair
A present he dare not open
For fear he has never wanted anything more.

*

Janis came in all shades of red
Snarling and stalking the streets
Intent on leaving teeth marks in my innocence

If

If I were a sound I'd be a cough
Involuntary but always urgent
If I were a colour it would be dark
The kind of colour that can stain things permanently
If I were a word I would trip over your tongue
Bang my consonants against the roof of your mouth
I would stick to your teeth like molten toffee
If I were a colouring pencil
I would stare at the gaping cave of a sharpener's blade
Weeping for every whittled inch stolen from me
If I were a song everyone would shout my chorus
And mumble my verses
If you asked me to dance I'd probably say yes
If I were a stripper I would take off all my clothes
Then continue stripping
Plucking my eyeballs from their sockets
Peeling my skin like PVA glue from fat fingers
I'd stand there red raw and pulsing
Demanding twenty pound notes be slid inside
The exposed bone of my ivory belt pelvis
If I were Elvis I'd have gone the whole hog
Covered my slowly rotting soul in rhinestones too
If I were a star I think I'd crumble
Under the weight of all those wishes
If I were braver I'd use the words
If maybe probably possibly a little less
If I were a poet
I don't think it would bring me happiness
But I would write and write and write
Praying my pen might snag its nib
On something shaped like it
Happiness that is
Such a lot of things to hang on one little word

I can only hope the thread they dangle by
Is much stronger than it looks

A Personal Malleable Manifesto

1. Reserve the right to be wrong at all times..

2. Do not seek to be the best. Seek to love it the most.

3. Laugh at yourself. You are ridiculous, after all.

4. Humble yourself. Stop being such an ardent, fawning member of the cult of *you*. When someone gets something you wanted for yourself, spit out the glass shards of pride in your throat and be happy for them. They probably worked just as hard as you, if not more so. Your moment will come soon enough and with that a scattering of battered egos. No victory is ever wholly sweet.

5. For every one thing you blame your parents for, there are twenty silent blessings they have given you that you are too young and graceless to comprehend.

6. Do not engage in conversations that make your skin feel tight and your heart weary. Do not sit down to lunch with girls who wish to lick at the carcass of your inner demons. Do not laugh at jokes plucked from the rotten fruit of malevolence and ignorance. Do not be seduced into saying things your tongue will never forgive you for. Make your vague excuses and walk away.

7. (I know it's hard sometimes. I know it's hard sometimes.)

8. Wear prom dresses to Sainsbury's and sequins to casual coffee dates. Don't wait for special occasions that will never come. Youth was made for bright colours and hemlines that hug upper thighs. Give your future elderly self something to smile fondly about.

9. Do you want or do you want to be wanted? Assess why your stomach flutters the way it does. Perhaps you are more in love with the view from the pedestal you have been placed on than the heartsick person who put you there.

10. As long as you still feel that singular seizure of joy in your stomach at the opening bars of Stevie Wonder's *Isn't She Lovely*, there's hope for you.

11. Opinions are made of putty, not concrete.

12. Observe. Never let your eyes go into auto pilot mode. It is a wicked and inexcusable waste of a weird and wonderful world.

13. Kisses are an urgent expression of something monumentous, not an inarticulate filler of awkward silences.

14. Ditto sex. You do not have to have sex to be sexy. Your patience will pay off. Clothes will melt off of their own accord under the right fingers.

15. We are all, for the most part and in the grand, soaring sweep of things, inconsequential. This fact will either weigh you down or make you airborne.

16. Count the small but improbable miracles. You've made it this far. Remember that. You've made it this far.

Thank You Ever So Much

Despite my occasional assertions of the contrary, it (life) cannot be done alone. I am only one little person and I am only as good as the company I keep. I am lucky enough to have a circle of people around me who radiate consistent beams of warmth, light, humour, kindness and wisdom. Any success or happiness I have is down to them and their tireless awesomeness. So to them, I say thank you. Thank you ever so much.

Clive – You are a beautiful, diligent soul. Thank you for all you have done for us spoken word folk. It is quiet revolutions like yours that truly change the course of the world. Remember to make time for your own glory too, though! I can't wait for your poetry collection.

Chew Tze Lin, Kavina Minhas and Rachel Schraer – When I'm in times of trouble, I always ask myself what you would do. The solution is inevitably in there somewhere. Thank you for all the long, long talks, the food, the hugs, the support in sticky times and your patient acceptance of my ridiculous and extensive neuroses. I am in awe of you. Though I'm wary of idolising people, I shall have to make an exception for you guys. I have a bottomless well of love for you all.

Sam Thomas - You are a silly, silly man and I love you. I'm your home girl for life. Shotgun performing a poem for your wedding.

The shiny, sexy Wandering Word Crew – You continuously inspire me. You are a talented, humble, crazy bunch of mavericks. Thanks for letting me join your gang.

Apples and Snakes – Stay on your grind! The work you do is amazing. Thank you for every gig, commission and tidbit of advice.

Tash Dummelow – Thanks for the site, the videos and the Twitter page. You relentless powerhouse, you. I want a front row seat for your inevitable takeover of the world.

22A – I highly doubt I will live with such an incredibly inspiring group of people again in my lifetime. Talk about peaking early! It was an honour to live in squalor with you.

9 Ground Floor Flat – The happiest of random occurrences brought us together under one roof. You are beautiful, each of you. THANKS.

FUZEes – You are my muses, you are my pals, you are my dancefloor mavericks. You lot make me feel alive – shine on.

To anyone who has ever supported my writing, ever – there aren't enough pages to name you all but please believe that I am radiating gratitude your way right now as we speak. Hit me up. I'll bake you cupcakes and write you an ode any time.

And finally, Mum – I don't have to always understand you to appreciate, love and revere you. Thank you will never suffice. I am proud of you. Persevere.

"The real value of a real education, which has almost nothing to do with knowledge, and everything to do with simple awareness; awareness of what is so real and essential, so hidden in plain sight all around us, all the time, that we have to keep reminding ourselves over and over: *This is water. This is water*."

David Foster Wallace

Lightning Source UK Ltd.
Milton Keynes UK
UKOW05f1446240417

299780UK00008B/324/P